Cereal TREATS

Printed in the United States of America
by G&R Publishing Co.

Distributed By:

507 Industrial Street
Waverly, IA 50677

ISBN 978-1-56383-508-7
Item #7110

Working hard in the kitchen?

Not at all!

But when you make these yummy treats, it'll look like it! In reality, you'll be in and out of the kitchen in no time.

Outrageously delicious!
Ridiculously easy!
That's the beauty of
Cereal Treats.

Snickers recipe, bottom of page

Basic Gooey Krispie Treats

Start With

½ C. butter

1 (16 oz.) bag marshmallows

7 C. *Rice Krispies* cereal

Melt butter and marshmallows together in a large saucepan. Stir in cereal and press into a greased 9 x 13" pan.

Beyond Basic

Add **Mix Ins**, **Toppings**, & **Sprinkles** from the next page.

*(**Snickers**, photo above: 8 fun-size Snickers candy bars chopped & mixed with cereal + 2 C. each chocolate chips & peanut butter chips, melted & spread on top + chopped peanuts sprinkled over all.)*

Take the Krispie Treats recipe beyond basic by mixing & matching from these columns to create your favorite flavor combo.

Mix Ins

Combine powders and wet ingredients with melted mixture before stirring in cereal and other Mix Ins.

- ¼ to ½ C. dry cake mix, cookie mix, or muffin mix
- 3 T. flavored gelatin powder
- 2 tsp. ground spice (like cinnamon) + 2 tsp. molasses or honey
- 2 T. nut butters (like P.B.)
- ¾ C. candy pieces (like M&Ms)
- 8 fun-size candy bars, chopped
- 2 C. crushed cookies (like Oreos)
- 2 C. baking chips (any flavor)
- 1 C. chopped yogurt- or chocolate-covered pretzels
- 1 C. malt powder + 1⅓ C. malted milk balls, crushed

Toppings

- melted baking chips, caramel bits, or almond bark
- nut butters
- whipped topping
- ice cream toppings

Sprinkles

- chopped nuts or candy
- crushed peppermints
- toffee bits
- decorating sprinkles
- coarse salt

try other cereal (like Trix)

cinnamon & molasses inside, cream cheese frosting on top

PB Rolo Balls

Ingredients

2 C. **Corn Flakes** cereal

2 T. sugar

¾ C. creamy peanut butter

⅓ C. light corn syrup

20 Rolo candies

1¼ C. semi-sweet chocolate chips

1½ T. vegetable shortening

Crush the cereal and pour it into a medium bowl. Add the sugar, peanut butter, and syrup; mix well.

Roll the mixture into 1½" balls and tuck a Rolo inside each one. Refrigerate for 30 minutes. No snitching!

Melt the chocolate chips and shortening together; stir until smooth. Dip the chilled balls into the chocolate until they're well coated, letting the excess drip off; set on waxed paper until the chocolate hardens. Then start poppin' them in your mouth. Scrumptious!

✔ **Note to Self:** *Instead of dipping the peanut butter balls in melted chocolate, try rolling them in powdered sugar. After they've set a few minutes, roll them again.*

Coconut Cream

Ingredients

- 2½ C. **Honey Nut Cheerios** cereal, divided
- 3 T. sugar
- ¼ C. butter, melted
- 1¼ C. milk or coconut milk
- 1 tsp. vanilla extract
- 1 (3.4 oz.) box coconut cream instant pudding mix
- ½ C. toasted coconut
- ½ C. whipped topping, thawed

Preheat your oven to 350°.

Crush cereal to make 1 cup and put it in a bowl with the sugar and butter; stir to blend. Press into the bottom of eight ramekins. Bake for 10 to 12 minutes or until just a little toasty-looking. Cool completely.

In a large bowl, whisk together milk, vanilla, and pudding mix until slightly thick. Stir in the coconut and whipped topping. Divide among the ramekins and smooth out over the crust. Chill at least 4 hours.

Garnish if you'd like.

✔ **Note to Self:** *Buy the coconut already toasted or toast it yourself by putting it in a baking pan in a 350° oven for 5 to 8 minutes or until it's a glorious golden color.*

Peanut Butter Éclair Bars

Ingredients

- 1 C. sugar
- 1 C. light corn syrup
- 2 C. peanut butter (crunchy or creamy)
- 8 C. Frosted Flakes cereal
- 1¼ C. butter, divided
- 4 C. powdered sugar
- 2 (3.4 oz.) boxes vanilla instant pudding mix
- ⅓ C. plus 1 T. milk
- 2 C. semi-sweet chocolate chips

creamy goodness

Get Started

Line a 10 x 15" rimmed baking sheet with greased foil.

Combine the sugar and syrup in a big saucepan. Bring to a boil and boil for 1 minute, stirring occasionally. Take the pan off the heat and stir in the peanut butter. Add cereal, stirring until those flakes are coated in syrup-y goodness. Spread in the prepped pan and press it down in there.

Melt ¾ cup butter; stir in the powdered sugar and both pudding mixes. Slowly stir in the milk until smooth and thick; spread over the crust.

Melt together the chocolate chips and the remaining ½ cup butter; spread over the pudding layer and chill.

Sweet-Tart Confetti Cups

sooo colorful

Ingredients

2 C. *Fruit Loops* cereal

1 (16.5 oz.) roll refrigerated sugar cookie dough

1 (8 oz.) block cream cheese, softened

1 (.22 oz.) pkg. Blue Raspberry Lemonade Kool-Aid powder

1 (7 oz.) tub marshmallow creme

1 C. whipped topping, thawed

Crushed, but still lookin' pretty!

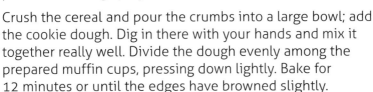

Get Started

Preheat the oven to 350°. Coat 12 cups of a regular-sized muffin pan with cooking spray.

Crush the cereal and pour the crumbs into a large bowl; add the cookie dough. Dig in there with your hands and mix it together really well. Divide the dough evenly among the prepared muffin cups, pressing down lightly. Bake for 12 minutes or until the edges have browned slightly.

Take the pan out of the oven and let set for 5 minutes. If the centers of the cookie cups haven't already sunk, press down on them gently with a spoon to form a cup. Run a small sharp knife around each cookie and carefully pop each one out of the pan. Let them set until they're cool enough to handle.

Beat together the cream cheese and Kool-Aid powder; add the marshmallow creme and mix thoroughly. Fold in the whipped topping. Transfer this mixture to a zippered bag; close the bag, snip off one corner, and pipe the filling into each cookie cup. Wasn't that fun? You can garnish them if you'd like or leave them as is.

Serve immediately or freeze for later.

Toasted S'mores

Ingredients

- 3 T. butter
- 4½ C. mini marshmallows, divided
- 4 C. Golden Grahams cereal
- 4 (1.55 oz.) milk chocolate candy bars, unwrapped

Get Started

Preheat the oven to broil. Grab an 8 x 8" baking pan and coat it with cooking spray.

In a large glass bowl, melt the butter in the microwave. Stir in 2½ cups of the marshmallows and microwave until melted and smooth, stirring occasionally. Stir in the cereal. Press this gooey mixture into the coated pan.

Lay the candy bars on top of the mixture in the pan. Press down on them gently to help them adhere. Toss on the remaining 2 cups of marshmallows.

Broil about 6" from the heat for a mere 1 to 2 minutes, keeping an eye on them so they don't burn. The marshmallows should be puffy and toasted and the chocolate should be soft. Mmm-mmm!

The hard part will be letting them set there until they're cool.

Cookie Delight

Ingredients

1 (16.5 oz.) roll refrigerated chocolate chip cookie dough

1½ qts. cookie dough ice cream, softened

2 C. Cookie Crisp cereal

½ C. fudge topping

Preheat the oven to 350°. Line a 9 x 13" baking pan with foil, letting the ends extend over the pan. Press the cookie dough evenly into the pan. Bake for 15 minutes, until golden brown; cool.

Spread the ice cream evenly over the crust. Top with cereal, pressing down lightly. Drizzle fudge topping over the cereal and freeze 1 hour or until firm. Best if eaten the same day.

It's cookie-licious!

✔ **Note to Self:** *Lifting up on those long foil ends and moving the dessert to a cutting board makes it easy to cut. And no more wrestling that first piece out of the pan.*

Ice Cream Crunch

Combine 2 C. crushed *Rice Chex*, ⅔ C. brown sugar, ½ C. chopped Spanish peanuts, and ½ C. sweetened flaked coconut. Drizzle with ½ C. melted butter and give it a stir; press half into an ungreased 9 x 13" pan. Cut ½ gallon of tin roof sundae ice cream into ¾" slices and arrange in the pan to cover the crust; smooth the top. Sprinkle the remaining crumb mixture over the top, pressing down lightly. Cover and freeze until firm. Crunchy, cold, and delightful! *Serves 24*

Chocolate-Covered Cherry Freeze

Line a 9 x 13" pan with buttered foil. In a saucepan, combine ½ C. butter, ¾ C. brown sugar, ½ C. light corn syrup, and ½ tsp. salt; bring to a boil. Remove from heat; stir in 5 C. *Crispix*, ¾ C. chopped walnuts, and ½ C. toffee bits. Scatter 1 C. of the cereal mixture on a plate and freeze; press remainder into the pan and freeze 10 minutes. Spread 1 qt. softened cherry ice cream over crust; freeze 30 minutes. Spread 1 qt. softened chocolate ice cream over cherry layer; sprinkle with remaining cereal mixture. Freeze 4 hours. Remove from pan to cut. Lip-smackin' good! *Serves 24*

Pumpkin-Praline Cheesecakes

Ingredients

- ¼ C. whole pecans
- ¼ C. brown sugar
- 2 T. heavy cream
- 2¾ C. *Cinnamon Toast Crunch* cereal, divided
- ¼ C. butter, melted
- 2 (8 oz.) blocks cream cheese, softened
- ¼ C. pumpkin puree
- ½ C. sugar
- 2 T. flour
- Pinch of salt
- ¼ tsp. pumpkin pie spice
- 1 tsp. clear vanilla extract
- ¼ C. plain Greek yogurt
- 2 eggs

delicious when toasted

Get Started

Preheat your oven to 350°.

Spray a baking pan with cooking spray.
Mix pecans, brown sugar, cream, and ¾ cup cereal and dump into the pan. Bake for 15 to 20 minutes or until nearly dry, stirring occasionally. Remove from the oven and set aside to cool. Reduce the oven temperature to 275°.

Finely crush the remaining 2 cups of cereal and mix with the butter. Set some pretty liners in 14 regular-sized muffin cups and divide the cereal-butter mixture among them.

Beat together the cream cheese, pumpkin puree, sugar, flour, salt, pumpkin pie spice, and vanilla until smooth and creamy. Add yogurt and eggs; mix until well combined, scraping down the side of the bowl as needed. Divide this mixture evenly over the crusts. Sprinkle each with a little of the pecan-cereal mixture. Bake for 20 to 25 minutes or until the edges of the cheesecakes are light golden brown and the centers still jiggle a little when you shake the pan. Let 'em cool in the pans on a wire rack until they reach room temperature then chill for a few hours.

A little bit of praline heaven.

Jumbo Raisin Crunchers

Ingredients

2 C. flour

1 tsp. baking powder

½ tsp. salt

¼ tsp. ground cinnamon

¾ C. butter, softened

⅔ C. sugar

⅓ C. brown sugar

1 egg

½ tsp. vanilla extract

1½ C. lightly crushed
Raisin Bran Crunch cereal

½ C. sweetened flaked
coconut

¾ C. raisins

½ C. chopped pecans

Get Started

Preheat your oven to 375°. Line two baking sheets with parchment paper.

Stir together the flour, baking powder, salt, and cinnamon. In a separate bowl, beat the butter until smooth and creamy. Add sugar and brown sugar and beat for 2 minutes. Beat in egg until well blended. With the mixer on medium-low speed, add vanilla. Then add the flour mixture a little at a time, beating until just incorporated.

Stir in the cereal, coconut, raisins, and pecans by hand. The dough will be thick. For each cookie, drop ¼ cup of dough on the prepared baking sheets and bake for 17 minutes or until the cookies are nice and brown.

Remove from the oven and let them set on the baking sheets for 2 minutes before transferring them to a cooling rack.

Cherry-Chocolate Pizza

Ingredients

1 (12 oz.) pkg. semi-sweet chocolate chips

3 C. white baking chips, divided

2 C. mini marshmallows

1 C. *Rice Krispies* cereal

1 C. *Cocoa Krispies* cereal

¾ C. chopped walnuts

½ C. halved maraschino cherries, drained

¼ C. sweetened flaked coconut

the perfect topper

Get Started

Grab a pizza pan and give it a spritz of cooking spray.

In a glass bowl, combine the chocolate chips and 2½ cups of white baking chips. Microwave until melted, stirring occasionally. Stir in the marshmallows, both cereals, and walnuts until everything is coated in chocolate bliss. Dump the mixture onto the waiting pan and spread evenly.

Arrange the drained cherry halves over the chocolate base and then sprinkle with coconut. Pop it in the refrigerator to set up.

Melt the remaining ½ cup of white baking chips and drizzle over the top of the chilled base.

Cut. Serve. Eat. Enjoy.

✔ **Note to Self:** *Place the cherry halves on paper towels to drain and pat them with additional paper towels to remove as much of the moisture as you can.*

Fall Harvest Bars

Ingredients

½ C. butter, softened

1 (15.25 oz.) box yellow cake mix with pudding

1 egg

3½ C. mini marshmallows

½ C. light corn syrup

¼ C. sugar

¼ C. brown sugar

½ C. creamy peanut butter

2 tsp. vanilla extract

2½ C. Crispix cereal

1½ C. dry roasted peanuts

1 C. candy corn

Get Started

Preheat your oven to 350°.

Beat together the butter, cake mix, and egg. When it starts to hold together like dough, press it into an ungreased 10 x 15" rimmed baking sheet and bake for 15 minutes or until the edges are a nice golden color.

Take the pan out of the oven and immediately put the marshmallows in a single layer on top of the crust. Put the pan back in the oven for 2 minutes or until the marshmallows are puffy; remove from the oven and set aside while you make the topping.

Combine the syrup, sugar, and brown sugar in a large saucepan; bring to a boil over medium heat, stirring often. Take the pan off the heat and stir in the peanut butter and vanilla until it's like a peanut butter pool. Stir in the cereal, peanuts, and candy corn until coated. Now, drop mounds of this hot stuff over the 'mallows and spread gently.

Delicious!

✔ **Note to Self:** *It works well to use wet hands to spread the cereal mixture over the marshmallows. When you're done, it's only fair that you get to lick your fingers!*

Puppy Chow

Simply Basic

Melt together ¼ C. butter, ½ C. creamy peanut butter, and 1 C. milk chocolate chips. Add to a big ol' bowl with 9 C. *Rice Chex* and stir to coat. Put 2½ C. powdered sugar in a large bag, add the cereal mixture, and shake it like crazy until the cereal pieces are coated. Dump out to cool. Toss in a handful of milk chocolate chips before serving. It's so "dog-gone" good! Makes 9 cups.

Snickerdoodle

Pour 6 C. *Rice Chex* into a big bowl. Melt 1¾ C. white baking chips and pour over the cereal, stirring to coat every cereal piece. Mix ¾ C. powdered sugar, ¼ C. sugar, and 2 tsp. ground cinnamon in a large bag. Add cereal mixture. Shake, shake, shake. Shake, shake, shake. Shake your baggie. Shake your baggie. Dump out to cool. Tastes just like the cookie it's named for! Makes 6 cups.

Cookies & Cream

Melt 1 C. white baking chips with 1 tsp. shortening; mix with 4½ C. *Crispex*. Finely crush 8 Oreos; mix half the crumbs with ¾ C. powdered sugar and stir into coated cereal. Dump out to cool. Melt 1 C. semi-sweet chocolate chips with 1 tsp. shortening; mix with 4½ C. *Crispex*. Mix remaining Oreo crumbs with ¼ C. powdered sugar and ½ C. chocolate milk powder; stir into chocolate-coated cereal. Dump out. When cool, combine both mixtures. Add some mini Oreos, if you'd like. Dig in! **Makes 9 cups.**

Mocha-Nut

Dissolve 1½ T. instant coffee granules in 1½ tsp. hot water. Add 1 C. semi-sweet chocolate chips and ¼ C. butter; melt in the microwave. Mix 2 C. pecan halves, 3 C. *Chocolate Chex*, 4 C. *Cinnamon Chex*, and 1 C. pretzels; add the chocolate mixture and stir. In a large bag, mix ½ C. powdered sugar and 1 C. chocolate milk powder; add cereal mixture and shake to coat. Dump out to cool and add some Heath Bar pieces. Makes 10 cups.

Puppy Chow

Snicker-Snicker Chow-Chow

In a big bowl, stir together 8 C. popcorn, 5 C. *Rice Chex,* and 3 C. *Vanilla Chex.* Melt together ½ C. butter and 6 Snickers candy bars (yes, you really do melt the candy bars), stirring occasionally. Stir this melted concoction into the cereal mixture until coated. Dump 1 C. of powdered sugar over the top and stir to blend. Dump out to cool. So good! Makes 16 cups.

Cherry Cheesecake

Melt together 1 (10 oz.) pkg. cherry baking chips and 1 tsp. shortening. Add 5 C. *Vanilla Chex* and stir to coat. In a large bag, mix 1 (3.4 oz.) box cheesecake instant pudding mix and ½ C. powdered sugar. Add coated cereal and shake until everything is evenly distributed. Dump out to cool. It's very cherry good! **Makes 5 cups.**

Choco-Mint

Melt 1½ C. semi-sweet chocolate chips and pour over 5 C. *Rice Chex*; stir to coat. Stir in 1 C. finely crushed thin chocolate-mint cookies. Toss with ¼ C. powdered sugar to coat; dump out to cool. Melt 1½ C. green mint baking chips and pour over 5 C. *Rice Chex* cereal; stir to coat. Toss with ¾ C. powdered sugar. Dump out to cool. When cool, mix the two. Stir in extra cookie pieces, if desired. Deliriously delicious! Makes 11 cups.

Luscious Lemon

Pour 8 C. *Rice Chex* in a large bag. Melt together 1 C. white candy melts, ¼ C. butter, and ½ C. lemon curd in a saucepan over low heat, stirring constantly; add to the cereal in the bag and shake vigorously to coat. Add 1½ C. powdered sugar and shake to coat again. Dump out to cool. Toss in some lemon candies and decorating sprinkles for good measure. Lemony good! Makes 8 cups.

Insanity Brownies

Ingredients

1 (19.8 oz.) box brownie mix

Oil, eggs, and water as shown on brownie mix box

½ C. coarsely chopped salted dry roasted peanuts

1 C. chopped Reese's Peanut Butter Cup minis

2 C. mini marshmallows

1½ C. semi-sweet chocolate chips

1½ C. creamy peanut butter

2 C. Rice Krispies cereal

Get Started

Beat together brownie mix, oil, eggs, and water, and bake in a 9 x 13" baking pan according to the directions on the brownie mix box. Don't turn off your oven after baking.

When you take the pan out of the oven, sprinkle the brownie base with peanuts, peanut butter cups, and marshmallows. Return the pan to the oven and bake 5 minutes more or until the marshmallows are puffy and brown. OK, you can turn off your oven now.

Melt together the chocolate chips and peanut butter; stir until the mixture is good and smooth. Add the cereal, stirring to coat. Spread this mixture over the baked marshmallow layer – careful so you don't disturb those precious toasted marshmallows.

Refrigerate at least 2 hours before you partake in this pan of insanely delicious treats.

Banana Pudding Triflettes

Ingredients

3 eggs

⅓ C. cornstarch

1 T. clear vanilla extract

¾ C. plus 3 T. sugar, divided

¼ tsp. plus a pinch of salt, divided

3½ C. whole milk, divided

½ (17 oz.) box *Cracklin' Oat Bran* cereal

3 T. butter, melted

1 C. heavy cream

2 T. powdered sugar

3 to 4 bananas

sliced is nice

Get Started

In a big bowl, whisk together the eggs, cornstarch, vanilla, ¾ cup sugar, and ¼ teaspoon salt. Whisk in ½ cup of milk until blended.

In a large saucepan, heat the remaining 3 cups of milk over medium heat until it begins to simmer. Be sure to stir it occasionally. Slowly pour ½ cup of the hot milk into the egg mixture while whisking quickly and constantly. Add another ½ cup of hot milk, whisking the same way. When it's mixed up really well, slowly pour the egg mixture from the bowl into the remaining simmering milk, whisking constantly while you pour. Cook over medium heat until big bubbles break on the surface. Whisk, whisk, whisk.

Transfer the pudding to a large bowl and press a piece of plastic wrap directly on the surface of the pudding. Refrigerate several hours or until it's chilled.

Finely crush the cereal in a food processor, then add the butter, a pinch of salt, and the remaining 3 T. sugar; process again until combined. Set aside.

Beat together the cream and powdered sugar on medium-high speed until stiff peaks form. Peel and slice the bananas.

Put 1 to 2 tablespoons of the cereal mixture in the bottom of eight individual trifle or dessert bowls. Add a layer of pudding, banana slices, and whipped cream. Repeat layers and top with any remaining cereal crumbs. Refrigerate for an hour or so and then eat immediately.

Mallow Scotchies

Ingredients

4 C. mini marshmallows

¼ C. butter

¼ tsp. salt

1⅓ C. butterscotch chips, divided

2 C. toasted coconut

4 C. *Corn Flakes* cereal

⅓ C. white baking chips

Marshmallow topping, optional

Coat an 8 x 8" pan with a bit of cooking spray.

In a big saucepan over medium-low heat, melt together the marshmallows, butter, and salt until velvety smooth, stirring often. Take the pan off the heat and stir in 1 cup of butterscotch chips. Keep on stirring until the chips are melted.

Quickly stir in the coconut and cereal. Then stir in the white baking chips and the remaining ⅓ cup butterscotch chips; spread evenly in the prepped pan. Cool until set for easiest cutting or cut immediately if you don't care and can't wait.

Drizzle with a little marshmallow topping, if you'd like.

Serious cereal-iciousness!

Jumbled Life Bars

Ingredients

Butter for greasing the pan, plus ¼ C. butter, cubed

2 C. popcorn

2 C. *Life* cereal

1 C. mini pretzel twists

1 C. plain M&Ms, divided

1 (10 oz.) bag mini marshmallows

Grease an 8 x 8" pan with butter.

In a big bowl, throw together the popcorn, cereal, pretzels, and ½ cup M&Ms.

Melt together the marshmallows and remaining ¼ cup butter, stirring until smooth. Pour over the cereal mixture and stir until all the pieces are well coated. Spread evenly in the waiting pan. Toss the remaining ½ cup M&Ms over the top and press down lightly.

Enjoy 'em soft and gooey.

Berry Icebox Pie

Ingredients

Butter for greasing the pan,
plus ¼ C. butter, melted

5 C. Cheerios cereal

¼ C. brown sugar

2 C. raspberries, blueberries,
and/or sliced strawberries

1 (14 oz.) can sweetened
condensed milk

2 egg yolks

1 C. whipped topping,
thawed

Get Started

Preheat your oven to 350°. Grease a 9" springform pan
with a bit of butter.

In a food processor, coarsely crush the cereal. Add brown
sugar and remaining ¼ cup butter; pulse to combine. Spread
in the bottom of the prepared pan, using the bottom of a
measuring cup to press firmly in place. Bake for 10 to 15
minutes or until golden brown. Cool completely.

Wipe out the food processor and dump in the fruit. Process
until smooth. Pour this into a medium bowl and refrigerate.

Meanwhile, in a small saucepan, whisk together the
sweetened condensed milk and egg yolks. Cook until the
mixture starts to steam, whisking often; do not let it boil.
Stir this into the chilled berry mixture and chill again.

Once the berry mixture is cool, spread it over the crust.
Spread the whipped topping over it and freeze several hours,
until set.

Peppermint Two-Tone Treats

Ingredients

11 T. butter, softened & divided

1 (10 oz.) bag regular marshmallows

3 C. *Rice Krispies* cereal

3 C. *Cocoa Krispies* cereal

⅓ C. semi-sweet chocolate chips

3¾ C. powdered sugar

3 to 4 T. milk

1⅛ tsp. peppermint extract

Green food coloring

3 oz. semi-sweet baking chocolate

two cereals
make 'em fun

Get Started

Line a 9" square pan with parchment paper, letting ends extend over pan.

In a big saucepan over low heat, melt 3 tablespoons of butter; add the marshmallows, stirring constantly until melted. Remove the pan from the heat and stir in both cereals and the chocolate chips. Press evenly into the prepared pan. Cool completely.

Blend together the powdered sugar and 6 tablespoons of the butter. Add 3 tablespoons of milk and beat until nice and creamy. Add the remaining tablespoon of milk, if needed, to make spreadable. Stir in the peppermint extract and enough food coloring to make a happy shade of green. Spread this minty concoction over the top of the cooled cereal mixture. Refrigerate an hour or so until firm.

Chop the baking chocolate and melt together with the remaining 2 tablespoons of butter. Spread quickly and evenly over the mint layer. Refrigerate again until the chocolate is set.

Lift up on the parchment paper to remove the treats from the pan before cutting.

Cookie Jacks

Ingredients

- ¼ tsp. ground cinnamon
- 1¾ C. sugar, divided
- 1 C. butter, softened
- 2 eggs
- 2¾ C. flour
- 1 T. baking powder
- ¼ tsp. salt
- 2 C. Apple Jacks cereal

cinnamon-apple O's

Get Started

Preheat your oven to 400°. In a small bowl, stir together the cinnamon and ¼ cup sugar.

In a large mixing bowl, beat together the butter and the remaining 1½ cups sugar until creamy. Beat in the eggs. Then add the flour, baking powder, and salt and mix just until combined. Stir in the cereal.

For each cookie, roll a heaping teaspoonful of dough into a ball, set on an ungreased baking sheet, and flatten slightly. Sprinkle each with a little of the cinnamon-sugar mixture. Bake for 8 to 10 minutes or until golden.

Take 'em out of the oven and hit 'em again with a little cinnamon-sugar. Let stand a minute before moving to a cooling rack.

Puffaroos

Ingredients

- 6 C. *Reese's Puffs* cereal
- 1 C. sugar
- 1 C. light corn syrup
- 1 (16.3 oz.) jar creamy peanut butter
- 1 C. semi-sweet or dark chocolate chips

Line a baking sheet with waxed paper. Pour the cereal into a big bowl.

In a medium saucepan, combine the sugar and syrup. Turn the stove to medium-high and bring the mixture a full boil, stirring the entire time. Take the pan off the heat and stir in the peanut butter. *(Yes, the whole jar. Go ahead. Don't be afraid.)* Pour this peanut buttery blend over the cereal in the bowl and stir, making sure to coat all of the cereal.

Scoop out some of the warm cereal mixture, form it into a 1½" ball, and place it on the baking sheet. Do that until the bowl is empty and the baking sheet is full. Scrape out any gooey-ness left in the bowl and just eat it.

Melt the chocolate chips and drizzle over the tops of the cereal balls. Refrigerate until set.

Delish!

Chexaroos

Stir together 6 C. *Rice Chex* and 1¼ C. salted dry roasted peanuts. In a saucepan, mix 1 C. brown sugar and 1 C. light corn syrup; bring to a boil over medium heat and boil for 1 minute. Remove from the heat and stir in 1 C. creamy peanut butter, 1 T. vanilla, and 1 tsp. salt. Pour this over the cereal mixture and stir to coat. Press the mixture gently into a greased 9 x 13" pan; let cool. Melt ¾ C. milk chocolate chips and drizzle over the bars. Yummy! *Serves 24*

Heatharoos

Combine 1 C. light corn syrup and 1 C. sugar in a saucepan over medium heat, stirring until it begins to boil and the sugar dissolves. Remove from heat and stir in 1 C. peanut butter. Stir in 6 C. *Rice Krispies*. Spread evenly in a greased 9 x 13" pan. Melt together 1¼ C. semi-sweet chocolate chips, ¾ C. butterscotch chips, and ¾ C. half & half or heath-flavored coffee creamer. Pour over the cereal mixture and sprinkle with 2 chopped Heath candy bars. Chill to set. Yahoo Heathroos! *Serves 24*

Surprise-Inside Snowballs

Ingredients

- 2 T. butter, plus more for greasing your hands
- 2 C. mini marshmallows
- 4 C. Cocoa Krispies cereal
- 10 regular marshmallows
- 12 to 14 oz. white baking chocolate, chopped
- 3 C. sweetened flaked coconut

Don't you just love surprises?

Get Started

Line a baking sheet with parchment paper.

Melt 2 tablespoons butter in a large saucepan over medium heat. Add the mini marshmallows and continue heating until melted and smooth, stirring often. Remove the pan from the heat and stir in the cereal until well coated. Let stand a few minutes until cool enough to handle.

Put a little bit of butter on your hands and shape a scant ½ cup cereal mixture around each regular marshmallow. Repeat until all the cereal mixture is used up. Let them rest until they're completely cool.

Melt the baking chocolate according to the package directions. Push a skewer into the center of a cereal ball and coat the ball with the melted white chocolate; sprinkle with lots of coconut. (Don't be shy – really pack that coconut on there so it holds.) Place the coated ball on waxed paper, remove the skewer, and repeat with the remaining balls. Let stand until the chocolate has hardened.

They're yummy AND fun!

1

2

3

4

① Apple-Cinnamon

In a large glass bowl, microwave ¼ C. butter, ⅓ C. brown sugar, 2 T. light corn syrup, and 1 tsp. cinnamon until boiling; stir in 5 C. *Wheat Chex* and 1 C. cashews. Microwave 3 minutes, stirring often. Stir in 1 C. chopped dried apples; microwave until apples just begin to brown, about 2 minutes. Dump out to cool, then toss in some yogurt-covered raisins. Makes 8 cups.

② Lucky Crunch

Melt 5 squares of white almond bark and let stand for 10 minutes. Stir in 2½ C. *Lucky Charms*, 1 C. dark chocolate M&Ms, 1 C. peanut butter-filled pretzel bites, and ½ C. dark chocolate chips. Dump out to cool. It's magical. It's delicious. Makes 5 cups.

③ Cap'n Crunchies

Combine 4 C. *Cap'n Crunch*, ½ C. nonfat dry milk, 2 T. brown sugar, 1 T. sugar, and a pinch of salt. Mix ½ C. melted butter with ½ tsp. vanilla and stir into cereal to coat. Spread on a rimmed baking sheet lined with parchment paper; bake at 275° for 25 minutes, until lightly browned. When cool, stir in some Reese's Pieces just for fun. Makes 4 cups.

④ Caramel Fusion

Mix 4 C. *Corn Chex*, 8 C. popcorn, 1 C. pretzels, and 1 C. pecans. In a saucepan over medium-low heat, bring ¼ C. butter, ½ C. brown sugar, and ¼ C. light corn syrup to a boil, stirring often. Cook 5 minutes without stirring. Off the heat, stir in ½ tsp. baking powder and ¼ tsp. vanilla. Stir into cereal mixture. Dump onto a greased rimmed baking sheet and bake at 250° for 30 minutes; stir once. Dump out to cool. Makes 15 cups.

Party Mix!

1

2

3

4

46

Ranch Hand Munch

1

In a big bowl, stir together 1 (7.5 oz.) box Bugles, 3 C. *Crispix*, 1 (6.6 oz.) bag Goldfish crackers, 1 (7 oz.) box white cheddar Cheez-Its, and 2 C. each pretzels and cashews. Slowly stir in ¾ C. popcorn oil and 1 (1 oz.) pkg. each ranch dressing mix and ranch dip mix. Divide the mixture between two large rimmed baking sheets; bake at 250° for 40 minutes, stirring occasionally. Makes 21 cups.

Easy Corn Poppers

2

Melt 7 T. butter in a large saucepan. Remove from the heat and stir in 6 T. grated Parmesan cheese and ¾ tsp. coarse black pepper. Add 3 C. *Corn Pops*, 2 C. corn chips, and 1 C. cashews, stirring until well coated. Sprinkle with coarse salt to taste. Makes 6 cups.

Wasabi Mix-Up

3

On a rimmed baking sheet, mix 2½ C. each *Cheerios* and *Spoon Size Shredded Wheat*, 2 C. oyster crackers, 7 C. popcorn, 1 C. unsalted dry roasted peanuts, and ½ C. wasabi dried peas. Stir together 1 T. Worcestershire sauce, 1 tsp. chili powder, 2 tsp. each salt, garlic powder, and onion powder, and 3 T. each honey and water; pour over the cereal mixture and stir to coat. Bake at 250° for 50 minutes, stirring occasionally. Makes 16 cups.

Spitfire Crunch

4

In a big bowl, mix 1½ C. *Kix*, 2 C. *Cheerios*, 1 C. *Corn Chex*, 1 C. corn nuts, ½ C. sunflower nuts, and 2 C. each mini bagel chips, Chili Cheese Fritos, and cheese-flavored Ritz Bitz. Melt 6 T. butter with 1 tsp. Worcestershire sauce, 1 tsp. garlic powder, 2 T. dried parsley flakes, ½ tsp. onion powder, ½ tsp. cayenne pepper, and 2 T. each green pepper sauce and hot sauce; stir into cereal mixture. Bake on a large rimmed baking sheet at 250° for 1 hour; stir occasionally. Makes 12 cups.

Frozen Banana Bites

Ingredients

6 bananas

Fruity Pebbles cereal

8 oz. dark chocolate chips

cut 'em up

roll gently

Get Started

Line a tray with waxed paper. Peel the bananas and cut each into thirds. Push a popsicle stick into one cut end of each chunk; set the chunks on the prepared tray and pop the tray in the freezer for at least 30 minutes.

Put the cereal on a plate. Microwave the chocolate chips in a microwave-safe cup until melted. Holding onto the stick, dip each banana chunk into the melted chocolate, letting the excess drip back into the cup. Roll immediately in the cereal and poke the stick into a sheet of Styrofoam until the chocolate dries. *(No Styrofoam? Just return them to the tray.)*

 melted white almond bark & crushed **Special K Red Berries**

Greek or vanilla yogurt & **Grape Nuts** *(refreeze briefly to harden yogurt)*

peanut butter (heated, if necessary) & **Honey Nut Cheerios** *(refreeze briefly to harden peanut butter)*

Chocolate Puff Cheesecake

serves 16

Ingredients

- 7 C. *Cocoa Puffs* cereal, divided
- ⅛ tsp. salt
- 10 T. butter, melted
- 3 (8 oz.) blocks cream cheese, softened
- 1½ C. powdered sugar

- 1 T. vanilla extract
- 8 oz. bittersweet baking chocolate, melted
- ¾ C. heavy cream, divided
- 4 oz. semi-sweet baking chocolate, chopped

Get Started

Coat a 9" springform pan with cooking spray. Finely crush 5 cups of the cereal; add salt and butter and mix until moistened. Press firmly into the bottom and 2" up the sides of the pan.

In a large bowl, beat the cream cheese until smooth. Add the powdered sugar and vanilla and beat until fluffy, scraping down the sides of the bowl while you mix. Add the bittersweet chocolate and beat until well combined. In a small bowl, beat ½ C. cream until soft peaks form; fold into the chocolate mixture. Spread this filling over the crust in the pan; chill for 1 hour. Hang on, there's more chocolate on the way.

In a double boiler, melt the semi-sweet baking chocolate with the remaining ¼ cup of cream, whisking until smooth. Let cool a few minutes and then spread over the cheesecake. Immediately scatter the remaining 2 cups of cereal over the top, pressing down lightly. Chill before slicing.

A chocolate-lover's dream!

Lemon Meringue Krispies

Ingredients

¼ C. butter

1 (16 oz.) bag mini marshmallows

1 (2.9 oz.) box lemon cook & serve pudding mix

8 C. *Rice Krispies* cereal

1 T. light corn syrup

⅔ C. plus 2 T. sugar, divided

3 egg whites, at room temperature

mallows make
cereal delicious

Get Started

Line a 9 x 9" baking pan with foil and coat lightly with cooking spray.

Melt the butter in a large saucepan. Add the marshmallows, stirring until melted. Stir in the pudding mix and then remove the pan from the heat. Stir in the cereal until it's all gooey. Press the mixture lightly into the prepped pan. Cool at least 20 minutes.

In a medium saucepan, combine syrup, ⅔ cup sugar, and 2 tablespoons of water; bring to a boil over medium heat. Attach your trusty candy thermometer to the saucepan and cook until the mixture reaches 230°, stirring occasionally. While you're waiting, beat the egg whites at high speed until foamy; gradually add the remaining 2 tablespoons of sugar, beating until soft peaks form.

When the hot sugar mixture is up to temperature, slowly drizzle it down the inside of the bowl containing the beaten egg whites; beat on medium speed until well mixed. Crank up the speed to high and beat for 7 minutes, until it's thick and glossy. Spread evenly over the cereal mixture.

Brown the meringue with a culinary torch. Serve these the same day for the best taste and texture.

✔ **Note to Self:** *No torch? No problem. Just place the pan under the broiler for 15 to 30 seconds or until lightly browned, watching carefully so the meringue doesn't burn.*

Chocolate Stud Cookies

makes 32

Ingredients

2 C. *Frosted Mini Wheats* cereal

½ C. butter, softened

½ C. sugar

½ C. brown sugar

1 egg

1 tsp. vanilla extract

1 C. flour

¼ tsp. salt

½ tsp. baking soda

½ tsp. baking powder

1 C. semi-sweet chocolate chips

Get Started

Preheat the oven to 350°. Lightly coat a baking sheet with cooking spray.

In a food processor, process cereal until finely ground *(you should end up with about 1 cup of cereal crumbs).*

In a large bowl, cream together butter, sugar, and brown sugar until well blended. Add the egg and vanilla; mix well.

In a bowl, stir together the flour, salt, baking soda, and baking powder; add this to the butter mixture and beat until it's all nicely blended. Stir in the cereal crumbs and chocolate chips. Drop by rounded tablespoonful onto the prepped baking sheet; bake for 12 to 15 minutes or until cookies are a nice golden brown. Take the pan out of the oven and let set 5 minutes before you remove the cookies to a cooling rack.

Crisp on the outside, chewy on the inside.

Honey Bunch Apple Crisp

Ingredients

2 C. *Honey Bunches of Oats with Almonds* cereal

¾ C. brown sugar

¼ C. sugar

⅓ C. flour

1 tsp. ground cinnamon

¼ C. butter, melted

4 Granny Smith apples, peeled, cored & sliced ½" thick

½ C. apple juice

⅓ C. sliced almonds

How 'bout them apples!

Get Started

Preheat the oven to 350° and coat a 9 x 9" baking pan with cooking spray.

Stir together the cereal, brown sugar, sugar, flour, and cinnamon. Add the butter and stir it all up. Toss 1½ cups of the cereal mixture with the apple slices and dump this into the prepared pan, spreading out those coated apples evenly. Drizzle the apple juice over the top. Bake uncovered for 30 minutes.

Stir the almonds into the remaining cereal mixture and spread this out over the apples. Bake uncovered 20 minutes more or until the apples are tender and the topping is nicely browned.

Delicious warm or cold, with or without ice cream. Try it, you'll love it!

✔ **Note to Self:** *Granny Smith apples add just the right amount of tart to this sweet dessert.*

Cinnamon Crunch Cupcakes

Ingredients

2 C. *Cinnamon Toast Crunch* cereal

1 T. ground cinnamon

1 (15.25 oz.) box vanilla cake mix

Oil, eggs, and water as shown on cake mix box

Your favorite frosting

Get Started

Preheat your oven to 350°. Set liners in 24 regular-sized muffin cups. Finely crush the cereal; add the cinnamon and mix well.

Stir together the cake mix, oil, eggs, and water as directed on the cake mix box. Fill the muffin cups ⅓ full with cake batter, then sprinkle each with about ½ teaspoon of the cinnamon-cereal mixture. Fill to ⅔ full with cake batter and sprinkle with the rest of the cinnamon-cereal. Run a fork through the batter to swirl. Bake for 15 minutes or until a toothpick comes out clean. Now, let these little gems cool.

Right before you're ready to serve, spread on some frosting and garnish any way you'd like.

They taste like light and airy little coffee cakes.

Cool Kat Bars

chop-chop-chop

Ingredients

1¼ C. creamy peanut butter, divided

½ C. sugar

¼ C. brown sugar

½ C. light corn syrup

1 T. vanilla extract

4 C. *Rice Krispies* cereal, divided

1 C. semi-sweet chocolate chips

2 or 3 (1.5 oz.) Kit Kat bars, diced

Get Started

Spray an 8" square pan with a bit of cooking spray.

Put 1 cup of the peanut butter in a large glass bowl. Dump in sugar, brown sugar, and syrup. Take it for a spin in the microwave for 1 minute and then give it a stir. Microwave 1 minute more, then stir in the vanilla and 3 cups of cereal until nicely coated. Put this mixture into the sprayed pan and really pack it in there; smooth the top.

Toss the chocolate chips and remaining ¼ cup peanut butter in the bowl you used before. Microwave until melted, stirring until smooth. Pour in the remaining 1 cup of cereal and stir until well coated. Now dump it over the base layer in the pan and spread it evenly in place.

Immediately begin setting the Kit Kat pieces on top, pressing into the chocolate so they stay in place. The candy pieces melt just a little bit, which helps them adhere and makes them extra delicious-looking. After the chocolate is nearly cool, refrigerate until firm.

My, oh my...

✔ **Note to Self:** *You can just toss the candy pieces on willy-nilly if you'd like, but placing them in rows makes for easier cutting.*

Fruit & Cereal Pizza

Ingredients

- 4 C. *Corn Flakes* cereal
- 2½ T. butter, softened
- 2 T. light corn syrup
- ¼ C. sugar, divided
- 1½ (8 oz.) blocks cream cheese, softened
- 1 (7 oz.) tub marshmallow creme
- Fruits of your choice, sliced & drained as needed

Get Started

Preheat your oven to 350°. Crush the cereal until it measures 1½ cups and dump it into a medium bowl. Add butter, syrup, and 2 tablespoons of the sugar; stir it all together until it's well blended. Press firmly into a 12" pizza pan using the bottom of a measuring cup if the mixture sticks to your hands.

Pop it in the oven and bake until the crust is a light golden brown color, about 5 minutes. Take it out of the oven and let it cool completely.

In a clean bowl, mix the cream cheese and marshmallow creme until it's super smooth and creamy. Spread it all over the cooled crust.

Arrange the fruit over the top and slide it in the refrigerator for an hour to set up a bit.

Index